21 Adventures

John D. Mac Donald's
TRAVIS McGEE SERIES

Travis McGee—star of twenty-one novels, every one
as good as the last—part rebel, part philosopher,
and every inch his own man. He is a rugged,
Florida beach bum with a special knack
for helping friends in trouble—or
avenging their deaths.

"McGee has become part of our national
fabric." *Seattle Post Intellegencer*

THE
OFFICIAL
TRAVIS McGEE
QUIZ
BOOK

John Brogan

FAWCETT GOLD MEDAL • NEW YORK

A Fawcett Gold Medal Book
Published by Ballantine Books

Copyright © 1984 by John Brogan

Library of Congress Catalog Card Number: 84-90881

ISBN 0-449-12709-2

Printed in Canada

First Ballantine Books Edition: July 1984
Fourth Printing: June 1988

To
Jane
for
1980

❖ Contents ❖

THE
OFFICIAL
TRAVIS McGEE
QUIZ
BOOK

GENUINE
❖ INTRODUCTION ❖

Good luck out there with this thing!

I didn't get a look at it until it was finished, and I know now that my suggestion didn't work. I told them (the editors) in the beginning that they should put out the basic quiz for ninety-five cents and then sell the answers separately for five dollars and ninety-five cents.

I would have had to buy the answers.

Memory is a very iffy thing, varying from person to person. I have a friend who has a little machine in his head that accepts any number of phone numbers and plays them back on request, but he forgets where he parked his car. Another friend can quote batting averages of ball players I never heard of, as far back as 1927. And he has yet to remember the birthday of his bride of twenty-four years.

My own memory is a social embarrassment. I simply cannot remember names, and I cannot remember faces. And so all social gatherings, except with the oldest and best friends, are painful. I avoid parties with the same ardor I avoid hangnails. I tend to wobble about with a vapid smile, nodding and beaming and saying, "Well, hello there. Hey. How you? Hello, ol' buddy. What's new with you, pretty lady?" Etc.

This quiz is full of names. I made up the names. I wrote them down and I invented the people that fit the names. In the normal course of events, I have—during the writing and re-writing and rewriting and rewriting and rewriting—gone over those named people and what they did in their particular McGee book perhaps twenty times prior to publication. So I read this quiz and stare in consternation at a question and ask myself, "Who in hell was Francine Benedict?"

I do pretty well on all the parts of the quiz which have nothing to do with names. Just as I can still sing "A Bicycle Built for Two" in Urdu, many years after I gave up residence as a guest of the Pentagon in India. Just as I can remember the page number and placement on the page of something I want to look up for the second time in a reference work.

How memory works is, I guess, as individual a thing as a thumb print. All of us bog down in some areas, and shine in others.

In these days of the popularization of trivia, I must confess to being pleased to see that the McGee books become in some sense generic by becoming a lengthy source of tiny facts. I have always had the feeling that I have been writing one very long book about T. McGee and Meyer, and this quiz seems to tie the package together.

Good luck with it. Have fun with it. I would be totally awed by anybody who could get more than 60% of these right the first time. I will not tell you my score. I will not *ever* tell you my score.

At this moment in time we are leaving for a couple of months in Mexico. I shall tote the partial manuscript of the twenty-first McGee, as yet untitled, and if my typewriter has not turned into a half bushel of rust since I left it there two years ago, I will finish the book down in the Yucatan.

John D. MacDonald
December 1983

Apprentice
Detective

❖ QUIZ 1 ❖

McGee Potpourri

1. What is the name of Travis McGee's houseboat?

   A. Straight Flush
   B. Acey Deucy

   C. Busted Flush
   D. Full House

2. What is Travis McGee's official occupation?

   A. Private investigator
   B. Writer

   C. Salvage Consultant
   D. Boat captain

3. What sport did McGee play when he met "Tush" Bannon?

   A. Football
   B. Baseball

   C. Basketball
   D. Wrestling

4. Name McGee's favorite liquor.

    A. Gin   C. Scotch
    B. Bourbon   D. Rye

5. What percentage of retrieved goods does McGee usually ask for his services?

    A. 10%   C. 50%
    B. 25%   D. 75%

6. In what state does Travis McGee reside?

    A. California   C. Florida
    B. Texas   D. Louisiana

7. What is the name of Travis McGee's car?

    A. The McGeemobile   C. The Salvager
    B. The Baron   D. Miss Agnes

8. What is McGee's theory on retirement?

    A. Save for it   C. Take it a little bit at
    B. Live for the present   a time
                        D. None of the above

9. What is wonderfully oversized on McGee's houseboat?

    A. Bed   C. Bathtub
    B. Water tanks   D. All of the above

10. How did McGee obtain ownership of his houseboat?

    A. As payment for ser-   C. As a gift
       vices   D. In a poker game
    B. From a horse race

❖ QUIZ 2 ❖

Meyer Potpourri

1. Meyer has a Ph.D. in what field?

   A. Economics
   B. Physics

   C. Mathematics
   D. Philosophy

2. What is the name of Meyer's boat that sank?

   A. The *John Stuart Mill*
   B. The *Albert Schweitzer*

   C. The *Longfellow*
   D. The *John Maynard Keynes*

3. How does Meyer earn a living?

   A. Stockbroker
   B. Writer

   C. Consultant
   D. Lawyer

4. What is Meyer's favorite game of skill?

    A. Bridge   C. Crossword puzzles
    B. Chess   D. Rubics cube

5. According to Meyer, what is the eighth deadly sin?

    A. Ignorance   C. Not voting
    B. Illiteracy   D. Being boring

6. In what McGee adventure did Meyer almost die?

    A. *The Turquoise La-*   C. *Free Fall in Crimson*
       ment   D. *The Empty Copper*
    B. *Cinnamon Skin*   *Sea*

7. Who or what are Meyer's "iron maidens"?

    A. Sure-fire investments   C. Lovers
    B. Twin antique pistols   D. Sailing crew

8. What characteristic of Meyer's always amazes Travis McGee?

    A. His seamanship   C. His wealth
    B. His ability to put   D. His athletic prowess
       people at ease

9. What description characterizes the Meyer Manifesto?

    A. A party resolution   C. Be a good neighbor
    B. Never break the law   D. Be loyal to friends

10. What occupation does Meyer sometimes put on his business cards?

    A. Certified guarantor   C. Importer-exporter
    B. Investment broker   D. Global investor

❖ QUIZ 3 ❖

True or false?

1. Meyer has a significant role in *The Quick Red Fox*.

2. Travis McGee is badly injured in *The Scarlet Ruse*.

3. In *Darker Than Amber*, Marathon refers to a boat McGee uses for a final escape.

4. In *Dress Her in Indigo*, El Tule refers to the world's largest tree.

5. The mystery in *One Fearful Yellow Eye* ultimately leads to the discovery of a Communist spy ring.

6. As *Dress Her in Indigo* opens, McGee and Meyer are headed back to Florida.

7. In *The Dreadful Lemon Sky*, McGee's boat is used to rescue refugees.

8. Norma Lawrence, Hacksaw Jenkins, and Pogo are all murder victims in *Cinnamon Skin*.

9. As used in *The Green Ripper*, the term "mole" refers to a traitor.

10. Bonnie Brae refers to McGee's girlfriend in *The Green Ripper*.

11. Travis McGee has an ex-wife living in Boston.

12. McGee's houseboat is impounded by the Coast Guard in *The Turquoise Lament*.

13. In *The Empty Copper Sea*, the Spanish explorer De Soto, the discoverer of Florida, is mentioned.

14. The call letters KVZK mentioned in *The Turquoise Lament* refer to McGee's radio call code.

15. The term "girls from Guadalajara" used in *Dress Her in Indigo* refer to names of Caribbean hurricanes.

❖ Quiz 4 ❖

Unscramble each of the following to reveal a McGee title.

1. INAOCNMN KNSI

2. HET RENGE PPIRRE

3. TEH DEDURAFL EOLMN KSY

4. EHT SALTCRE RSUE

5. EHT GONL REDNEVAL KLOO

6. ETH LRIG NI TEH AILNP RBWON PRWAERP

7. EON ERFALFU LYEOWL YEE

8. RGTBIH OERGNA ROF ETH HODUSR

9. EHT KCIQU DER XFO

10. TIHMRNGAE NI KPNI

❖ QUIZ 5 ❖

1. From what was Meyer suffering in *Cinnamon Skin*?

   A. Broken leg
   B. Bullet wound
   C. Financial problems
   D. Depression

2. In what branch of the military did Junior Allen serve?

   A. Marines
   B. Navy
   C. Army air corps
   D. Coast guard

3. In *The Long Lavender Look*, what was King Sturnevan's profession before becoming a police officer?

   A. Construction worker
   B. Football player
   C. Boxer
   D. Lawyer

4. On what historical anniversary does *The Green Ripper* begin?

   A. Fourth of July   C. The Bicentennial
   B. Bastille Day   D. Pearl Harbor day

5. In *The Empty Copper Sea*, the terms "hog," "crystal," "peace pill," "blasting powder," and "sugarino" are used. What do these terms describe?

   A. Nicknames   C. Dances
   B. Music   D. Drugs

6. During his reconnaissance of the Menterez compound in *A Deadly Shade of Gold*, what or who attacks McGee?

   A. Armed sentries   C. A lion
   B. Killer baboons   D. A guard dog

7. In *The Girl in the Plain Brown Wrapper*, McGee is the object of a Continental 0011. Identify this device.

   A. Handgun   C. Computer
   B. Experimental drug   D. Phone bug

8. Where was the movie mentioned in *Free Fall in Crimson* being shot?

   A. Iowa   C. Mexico
   B. Florida   D. Europe

9. Name the south pacific island McGee flys to in *The Turquoise Lament*.

   A. New Zealand   C. Truk
   B. Guadacanal   D. Samoa

10. What is McGee referring to in the following quote from *Nightmare in Pink*? "I could not imagine there would be more than three truly expensive circuits in the city."

    A. Drug rings   C. Call girls
    B. Mafia families   D. Labor unions

11. What desert denizen endangers McGee in *A Purple Place for Dying*?

    A. Gila monster   C. Rattlesnake
    B. Black widow spider D. Coyote

12. In what city is McGee arriving as *One Fearful Yellow Eye* opens?

    A. Chicago   C. San Francisco
    B. Miami   D. New Orleans

13. Who kills Tush Bannon in *Pale Gray for Guilt*?

    A. Freddy Hazzard   C. Gary Santo
    B. Preston LaFrance   D. He commits suicide

14. Who maintains the longest floating house party in the world?

    A. Meyer   C. The Alabama Tiger
    B. McGee   D. Chookie McCall

15. What large Texas city do McGee and Meyer visit in *Cinnamon Skin*?

    A. Houston   C. Fort Worth
    B. Dallas   D. Amarillo

❖ QUIZ 6 ❖

1. What type of oriental artifact is sold by Larry Joe Harris in *Cinnamon Skin*?

    A. Chinese vases
    B. Japanese lanterns
    C. Bamboo furniture
    D. Korean pottery

2. What is Lysa Dean famous for in *The Quick Red Fox*?

    A. Acting
    B. Modeling
    C. Dancing
    D. Philanthropy

3. From what country is Ulka Atlund in *The Quick Red Fox*?

    A. Norway
    B. Denmark
    C. United States
    D. Sweden

4. In *The Scarlet Ruse*, what expertise characterizes Hirsh Fedderman?

   A. Foreign affairs   C. Foreign languages
   B. Stamps   D. Chess

5. From what country is gold smuggled in *The Deep Blue Good-by*?

   A. Brazil   C. United States
   B. China   D. South Africa

6. What unusual attribute does Lilo Perris possess in *The Long Lavender Look*?

   A. Acute eyesight   C. Athletic prowess
   B. Extraordinary   D. Speech impediment
      strength

7. What crime is Lysa Dean a victim of in *The Quick Red Fox*?

   A. Murder   C. Embezzlement
   B. Blackmail   D. Smuggling

8. What cover does McGee use to infiltrate a cultist group in *The Green Ripper*?

   A. Potential recruit   C. Looking for his run-
   B. Mercenary   away daughter
                   D. Research for book

9. In *The Deep Blue Good-by*, who is Dads?

    A. Junior Allen   C. McGee
    B. Meyer   D. None of the above

10. Whose body does McGee find in Betsy Kapp's car in *The Long Lavender Look*?

    A. Lilo Perris   C. Lew Arnstead
    B. Henry Perris   D. King Sturnevan

11. What was the name of Van Harder's boat in *The Empty Copper Sea*?

    A. *Ocean Traveler*   C. *Neptune*
    B. *Charter King*   D. *Queen Bee III*

12. Name John Tuckerman's sister in *The Empty Copper Sea*.

    A. Kristin Petersen   C. Cathy Kerr
    B. Billy Jean Bailey   D. Gretel Howard

13. What was the name of Junior Allen's boat in *The Deep Blue Good-by*?

    A. *Play Pen*   C. *Golden Bough*
    B. *Bedazzled*   D. *Star*

14. Who tries to kill McGee in the first chapter of *A Tan and Sandy Silence*?

    A. Gavin Lee   C. Carl Brego
    B. Harry Broll   D. Dave Bellamy

15. Who was Hubbard Lawless's girlfriend in *The Empty Copper Sea*?

    A. Kristin Petersen   C. Tina Barton
    B. Tracy Smith   D. Gretel Howard

❖ QUIZ 7 ❖

1. What was the common fate of Hubbard Lawless and Kristin Petersen in *The Empty Copper Sea*?

   A. Murder victims C. Lost at sea
   B. Imprisoned D. McGee benefactors

2. What Caribbean island does McGee visit in *A Tan and Sandy Silence*?

   A. St. Croix C. Jamaica
   B. St. Kitts D. Grenada

3. What does The Doll House refer to in *Darker Than Amber*?

   A. A boutique C. A movie
   B. A brothel D. A toy store

4. Who impersonates Mary Broll in *A Tan and Sandy Silence*?

   A. Lisa Dissat   C. Mia Cruikshank
   B. Jeannie Dolan   D. Caroline Stoddard

5. To what Mexican town does McGee's investigation take
   him in *A Deadly Shade of Gold*?

   A. Mexico City   C. Puerto Altamura
   B. Acapulco   D. Baja City

6. In *A Tan and Sandy Silence*, what is the Hell's Belle?

   A. A boat   C. A lighthouse
   B. A bar   D. A condominium

7. To whom is Travis McGee referring in the following quote
   from *Darker Than Amber*? "...acquire people the way
   blue serge picks up lint..."

   A. Evangeline Bellemer C. Himself
   B. Merrimay Lane   D. Meyer

8. Who ends up cruising with McGee on his houseboat at the
   conclusion of *A Tan and Sandy Silence*?

   A. Lisa Dissat   C. Shannon McQuire
   B. Tami Western   D. Jeannie Dolan

9. From what malady is Carlos Menterez suffering in *A Deadly
   Shade of Gold*?

   A. Stroke   C. Polio
   B. Diabetes   D. Blindness

10. Who is *The Girl in the Plain Brown Wrapper*?

    A. Penny Woertz   C. Maureen Pearson
    B. Helen Pearson   D. Bridget Pearson

11. How was Nora Gardino killed in *A Deadly Shade of Gold*?

    A. Boat explosion   C. Plane crash
    B. Car accident   D. Train wreck

12. Who are the "girls" in the following quotation from *The Girl in the Plain Brown Wrapper*? "Also the girls are known to come screaming up . . . after the season is over."

    A. College girls   C. Hurricanes
    B. Out-of-state boaters   D. Drug smugglers

13. Who was Meyer's romantic involvement in *Free Fall in Crimson*?

    A. Sarah Black   C. Lysa Dean
    B. Millicent Waterhawk   D. Aggie Sloane

14. What is a Krugerrand as referred to in *Free Fall in Crimson*?

    A. An African dialect   C. A Dutch airline
    B. Currency   D. A parliamentary body

15. In *Free Fall in Crimson*, who or what are Preach, Magoo, Knucks, and Dirty Bob?

    A. Slang terms for drugs   C. Motorcycle club
    B. Slang for police   members
                        D. Code words

❖ QUIZ 8 ❖

1. In what business is Arts and Talents Associates in *Nightmare in Pink*?

   A. Theatrical agents   C. Call girls
   B. Stunt coordinators   D. Sports agents

2. Identify the term *goma* from *Dress Her in Indigo*.

   A. Marijuana   C. Opium
   B. Cocaine   D. Poisonous plant

3. In a legal sense, what unusual thing happens to McGee in *A Purple Place for Dying*?

   A. He gets married   C. He is arrested
   B. He is deputized   D. He gets sued

4. According to McGee, what is the "Mexican plague" in *Dress Her in Indigo*?

A. Motor scooters   C. Smog
B. Dysentery   D. Economic instability

5. In *A Purple Place for Dying*, in what southwestern state is Cotton Corners located?

A. New Mexico   C. Arizona
B. Texas   D. Unspecified

6. What crime did Jack Omaha commit in *The Dreadful Lemon Sky*?

A. Drug smuggling   C. Murder
B. Tax evasion   D. Kidnapping

7. Who is McGee trying to locate in *Dress Her in Indigo*?

A. Eva Vitrier   C. Meyer
B. Beatrice Bowie   D. Wally McLeen

8. In what unusual way does Fred Van Horn die in *The Dreadful Lemon Sky*?

A. Allergic reaction to   C. Electrocuted
    ant bites   D. Hit by lightning
B. Buried alive

9. What was Eva Vitrier's relationship with Beatrice Bowie in *Dress Her in Indigo*?

A. Sister   C. Lover
B. Mother   D. Sworn enemy

10. In *A Purple Place for Dying*, for what was Jasper Yeoman under investigation?

A. Murder   C. Racketeering
B. Conspiracy   D. Tax evasion

11. What old friend of McGee's shows up unexpectedly at his houseboat in *The Dreadful Lemon Sky*?

A. Carrie Milligan   C. Chookie McCall
B. Meyer   D. Arthur Wilkinson

12. What nationality is Eva Vitrier in *Dress Her in Indigo*?

A. Spanish   C. Greek
B. Italian   D. French

13. In what small Florida town does the action in *The Dreadful Lemon Sky* take place?

A. Biscayne City   C. Naples
B. Bayside   D. Deadman's Bay

14. To what does Jacksonville Hatteras refer in *The Dreadful Lemon Sky*?

A. A hurricane   C. An inland waterway
B. A flood   D. A cabin cruiser

15. What do Carrie Milligan, Joanna Freeler, Betty Joller, Chris Omaha, and Susan Dobrovsky have in common in *The Dreadful Lemon Sky*?

   A. Murder victims   C. A mutual lover
   B. Friends of McGee   D. Clients of McGee

❖ QUIZ 9 ❖

1. By whose request did McGee undertake a salvage operation in *One Fearful Yellow Eye*?

   A. Susan Kemmer
   B. Gloria Geis
   C. John Andrus
   D. Meyer

2. Identify Hero from *Pale Gray for Guilt*.

   A. War buddy of McGee's
   B. Marina roué
   C. Meyer's new boat
   D. City in Florida

3. What was Anna Ottlo's political background in *One Fearful Yellow Eye*?

   A. Communist
   B. Red Brigade
   C. Socialist
   D. Nazi

4. Who takes an overdose of LSD in *One Fearful Yellow Eye*?

   A. Meyer
   B. Anna Ottlo
   C. Heidi Trumbill
   D. Gloria Geis

5. What con was used against Arthur Wilkinson in *Bright Orange for the Shroud*?

   A. Land scam
   B. Inheritance fraud
   C. Stock swindle
   D. Tax scam

6. What was Anna Ottlo's relationship to Gloria Geis in *One Fearful Yellow Eye*?

   A. Maid
   B. Mother
   C. Daughter
   D. Business partner

7. In *One Fearful Yellow Eye*, she is divorced and an artist. Who is she?

   A. Janice Stanyard
   B. Mildred Shottle-hauster
   C. Gretchen Geis
   D. Heidi Trumbill

8. According to McGee, what city has "one of the great pipe stores of the Western world?"

   A. Washington, D.C.
   B. Los Angeles
   C. Chicago
   D. Boston

9. Identify Old Ugly from *Pale Gray for Guilt* .

    A. McGee   C. Mary Smith
    B. Tush Bannon   D. Meyer

10. What did Heidi Trumbill send McGee as a gift in *One Fearful Yellow Eye*?

    A. A dog   C. A painting
    B. A car   D. A book

11. What is the English meaning of *muñequita*?

    A. Fast one   C. Little doll
    B. Lovely sunset   D. Flower

12. Who is Poo Bear in *Pale Gray for Guilt*?

    A. Meyer   C. McGee
    B. Mary Smith   D. Connie Alvarez

13. What is Boone Waxwell's favorite fighting method in *Bright Orange for the Shroud*?

    A. Karate   C. Knifing
    B. Boxing   D. Kicking

14. Identify Connie Alvarez by occupation in *Pale Gray for Guilt* .

    A. Banker   C. Charterboat captain
    B. Orange grove owner   D. Oil tycoon

15. In *A Purple Place for Dying*, who or what are the Purity girls?

   A. Prostitutes
   B. Female softball team
   C. Sorority sisters
   D. Female bowling team

1. All of the following except one took part in defrauding Arthur Wilkinson in *Bright Orange for the Shroud*. Name this person.

    A. Chookie McCall
    B. Boone Waxwell
    C. Wilma Ferner
    D. Calvin Stebber

2. What is Annie Renzetti's occupation in *Cinnamon Skin*?

    A. Charter-boat captain
    B. Dance instructor
    C. Physician
    D. Hotel manager

3. What is the fate of Boone Waxwell in *Bright Orange for the Shroud*?

    A. Is captured by police
    B. Escapes
    C. Is killed
    D. Vanishes in swamp

4. What is a Bodyguard in *Darker Than Amber*?

    A. A security man   C. A handgun
    B. An armored vehicle   D. A modeling agency

5. Who do Travis McGee, Arthur Wilkinson, and Chookie McCall impersonate in *Bright Orange for the Shroud*?

    A. FBI agents   C. IRS agents
    B. TV technicians   D. Phone company repairmen

6. Whose suicide does McGee use to set the police on to Boone Waxwell's trail in *Bright Orange for the Shroud*?

    A. Vivian Watts   C. Debra Brown
    B. Arthur Wilkinson   D. Crane Watts

7. Who shoots McGee in *Bright Orange for the Shroud*?

    A. Crane Watts   C. Boone Waxwell
    B. Debra Brown   D. Frank Durkin

8. What do the terms Uzi and Kalashnikov refer to in *The Green Ripper*?

    A. Group leaders   C. Guns
    B. Russian advisers   D. Code words

9. What is the name of the small Florida town in which the action in *The Empty Copper Sea* takes place?

A. Everglades   C. Timber Bay
B. Canaveral City   D. Baytown

10. What is Billy Jean Bailey's occupation in *The Empty Copper Sea*?

    A. Dancer   C. Nurse
    B. Piano player   D. Karate instructor

11. What is Connie Melgar's nationality in *A Deadly Shade of Gold*?

    A. Cuban   C. Mexican
    B. Venezuelan   D. American

12. What kind of club did Rick Tate belong to in *Free Fall in Crimson*?

    A. Political   C. KKK
    B. Hunting   D. Motorcycle

13. What does the Lauderdale Bystander refer to in *The Turquoise Lament*?

    A. A social club   C. A newspaper
    B. A yacht   D. A tourist hotel

14. Identify the Plastics King in *Free Fall in Crimson*.

    A. Ellis Esterland   C. Prescott Mullen
    B. Peter Kesner   D. Harry Purcell

15. What long-running TV show is mentioned in *Cinnamon Skin*?

    A. *Gunsmoke*   C. *Archie Bunker's*
    B. *Mission Impossible*   *Place*
                               D. *M*A*S*H*

Super
Sleuth

❖ QUIZ 1 ❖

True or false?

1. In *Dress Her in Indigo*, Travis McGee describes himself as a "true eccentric."

2. Azteca Royale refers to an exotic Spanish dancer in *Cinnamon Skin*.

3. The name "Quimby" in *The Quick Red Fox* refers to a slang term for drug smugglers.

4. Junior Allen escapes retribution in *The Deep Blue Goodby*.

5. The character Gretel Howard appears in more than one McGee adventure.

6. Sam Dickey practices law in *Darker Than Amber*.

7. Ted Lewellen's specialty in *The Turquoise Lament* is oceanography.

8. Travis McGee is drugged with PCP in *Nightmare in Pink*.

9. 1500 in *The Dreadful Lemon Sky* refers to a coded phone number.

10. In *Dress Her in Indigo*, a *zocalo* refers to a drug.

11. Travis McGee is prematurely declared dead in *Cinnamon Skin*.

12. In *The Green Ripper*, Meyer uses a helicopter to rescue McGee.

13. McGee and Meyer are evicted from their marina in *Free Fall in Crimson*.

14. The nicknames Squeakie and Whippy refer to characters in *The Quick Red Fox*.

15. Travis McGee's sister becomes a client of his in *The Empty Copper Sea*.

❖ QUIZ 2 ❖

Match the Travis McGee book title with its date of publication.

1. *The Deep Blue Good-by*   A. 1964
2. *The Empty Copper Sea*   B. 1965
3. *One Fearful Yellow Eye*   C. 1966
4. *The Green Ripper*   D. 1968
5. *Bright Orange for the Shroud*   E. 1969
6. *Free Fall in Crimson*   F. 1970
7. *Pale Gray for Guilt*   G. 1978
8. *Cinnamon Skin*   H. 1979
9. *Dress Her in Indigo*   I. 1981
10. *The Long Lavender Look*   J. 1982

❖ QUIZ 3 ❖

Match the person with the Travis McGee book in which they appear.

1. Gretel Howard	A.	*Cinnamon Skin*
2. Tush Bannon	B.	*The Green Ripper*
3. Linda Brindle	C.	*The Scarlet Ruse*
4. Arthur Wilkinson	D.	*The Turquoise Lament*
5. Van Harder	E.	*The Quick Red Fox*
6. Harry Broll	F.	*Bright Orange for the Shroud*
7. Sam Taggart	G.	*A Deadly Shade of Gold*
8. Lysa Dean	H.	*The Empty Copper Sea*
9. Hirsh Fedderman	I.	*A Tan and Sandy Silence*
10. Norma Greene	J.	*Pale Gray for Guilt*

❖ QUIZ 4 ❖

Match the Travis McGee book with its main locale.

1. *The Quick Red Fox*
2. *A Deadly Shade of Gold*
3. *One Fearful Yellow Eye*
4. *Bright Orange for the Shroud*
5. *Cinnamon Skin*
6. *A Tan and Sandy Silence*
7. *The Green Ripper*
8. *Free Fall in Crimson*
9. *A Purple Place for Dying*
10. *The Turquoise Lament*

A. South Pacific
B. Los Angeles
C. Esmerelda
D. Mexico
E. Iowa
F. Chicago
G. California
H. Everglades
I. Grenada
J. Texas/Mexico

❖ QUIZ 5 ❖

1. Who is brought to justice by McGee and Meyer in *Cinnamon Skin*?

   A. Evan Lawrence
   B. Rowland Service

   C. Norma Greene
   D. Juan Torrez

2. What is Gabe Marchman's specialty in *The Quick Red Fox*?

   A. Firearms
   B. Photography

   C. Computers
   D. Law enforcement

3. What unusual fighting technique does McGee employ in *The Long Lavender Look*?

   A. Judo
   B. Sumo wrestling

   C. Karate
   D. Knife throwing

4. Name the town bully in *The Empty Copper Sea*.

    A. Hubbard Lawless   C. Van Harder
    B. John Tuckerman   D. Nicky Noyes

5. What alias does McGee use in *A Tan and Sandy Silence*?

    A. Stub Allen   C. Rupert Turner
    B. Gavin Lee   D. Lyle Kline

6. What was Jason Breen's motive for murder in *The Dreadful Lemon Sky*?

    A. Money   C. Insanity
    B. Love   D. Jealousy

7. In *A Deadly Shade of Gold*, in what Eastern European country is Shaja's husband imprisoned?

    A. Poland   C. Bulgaria
    B. Hungary   D. East Germany

8. For what purpose is the drug puromycin used in *The Girl in the Plain Brown Wrapper*?

    A. Memory loss   C. Blood pressure
    B. Sleep   control
                    D. Poison

9. In *The Turquoise Lament*, what kind of business is Seven Seas, Limited?

A. Import-export   C. Resorts
B. Fishing   D. Treasure hunting

10. To what important social problem does McGee allude in *Nightmare in Pink*?

    A. Drug addiction   C. Poverty
    B. Crime   D. Overpopulation

11. Whose life does McGee save in *A Purple Place for Dying*?

    A. Isobel Webb   C. Dolores Estobar
    B. Meyer   D. John Webb

12. What was Evangeline Bellemer's alias in *Darker Than Amber*?

    A. Angie Jones   C. Cleo Sanchez
    B. Kathy Philips   D. Tami Western

13. Who was Mary Smith representing in *Pale Gray for Guilt*?

    A. Preston LaFrance   C. Tush Bannon
    B. McGee   D. Gary Santo

14. Who almost ended the longest-running floating house party in the world in *Bright Orange for the Shroud*?

    A. Debra Brown   C. Vivian Watts
    B. Wilma Ferner   D. Meyer

15. What is Mrs. Simmons Davis in *Cinnamon Skin*?

    A. Eyewitness to crime   C. Murder victim
    B. McGee relative   D. Police informer

❖ QUIZ 6 ❖

1. What is Laura Honneker's profession in *Cinnamon Skin*?

   A. Psychiatry   C. Law
   B. Dentistry   D. Accountancy

2. Name Norma Greene's employer in *Cinnamon Skin*.

   A. Travis McGee   C. An oil company
   B. A state senator   D. A bank

3. What is Lysa Dean's real name in *The Quick Red Fox*?

   A. Lee Shontz   C. Gail Day
   B. Millie Homaker   D. Helen Schroeder

4. Who kills Mary McDermit in *The Scarlet Ruse*?

A. Albert Denton C. Frank Sprenger
B. Hirsh Fedderman D. Unknown

5. Name Norma Greene's attorney in *Cinnamon Skin*.

   A. Ted Post C. Roger Windham
   B. Davis Lewis D. Tony Vitelli

6. Who or what is Skeeter in *The Quick Red Fox*?

   A. A video game C. A board game
   B. An artist friend of D. A boat
      McGee

7. What is Mr. Goodbread's occupation in *The Scarlet Ruse*?

   A. Mobster C. Police officer
   B. McGee operative D. Stamp consultant

8. What U.S. vice-president is mentioned in *Cinnamon Skin*?

   A. John Nance Garner C. Richard Nixon
   B. Walter Mondale D. Lyndon Johnson

9. What is Evan Lawrence's real name in *Cinnamon Skin*?

   A. Jonathon Caster C. Cody Pittler
   B. Elliot Black D. Jasper Shute

10. Identify *Winds of Chance* from *The Quick Red Fox*.

    A. A movie C. A boat
    B. A sequel to the *Winds* D. A documentary
       of War

11. How was McGee injured in *The Quick Red Fox*?

    A. Shot   C. Hit on head
    B. Hit by car   D. Stabbed

12. What unusual item did McGee install aboard his houseboat in *The Scarlet Ruse*?

    A. A burglar system   C. Armor plating
    B. Two-way glass   D. A computer

13. Who was switching valuable stamp albums for fake ones in *The Scarlet Ruse*?

    A. Jane Lawson   C. Hirsh Fedderman
    B. Mary McDermit   D. Frank Sprenger

14. To what adolescent trauma of Evan Lawrence is there an allusion in *Cinnamon Skin*?

    A. Child abuse   C. Incest
    B. A car accident   D. A fire

15. What is Caswell Edgars's profession in *The Quick Red Fox*?

    A. Airline pilot   C. Artist
    B. Teacher   D. Private detective

❖ QUIZ 7 ❖

1. How did McGee get a lifetime membership at the exclusive Royal Biscayne Yacht Club in *The Scarlet Ruse*?

   A. Family connections   C. Inheritance
   B. Reward   D. Gift

2. What Academy Award-winning movie is mentioned in *The Scarlet Ruse*?

   A. *The French Connec-*   C. *The Sting*
      tion   D. *In The Heat of the*
   B. *The Godfather*   *Night*

3. What does McGee use to trick Junior Allen in *The Deep Blue Good-by*?

· 53 ·

A. Girlfriend   C. Precious gem
B. Valuable painting   D. Gold bullion

4. Who was operating a prostitution ring in *The Long Lavender Look*?

A. Lilo Perris   C. Henry Perris
B. King Sturnevan   D. Lew Arnstead

5. Who kills Lois Atkinson in *The Deep Blue Good-by*?

A. George Brill   C. David Berry
B. Junior Allen   D. Cathy Kerr

6. What is Davey Hoople's expertise in *The Scarlet Ruse*?

A. Mechanics   C. Sports medicine
B. Finances   D. Photography

7. Who victimized Cathy Kerr in *The Deep Blue Good-by*?

A. Junior Allen   C. Joe True
B. Jamie Hasson   D. William Callowell

8. Who is responsible for beating Meyer in *The Long Lavender Look*?

A. Lew Arnstead   C. Foster Goss
B. King Sturnevan   D. Fortner Geis

9. In what country did Meyer attend an economic conference in *The Green Ripper*?

A. Canada   C. Chile
B. Switzerland   D. Mexico

10. Who kills Lilo Perris in *The Long Lavender Look*?

    A. Henry Perris   C. Frank Baither
    B. Lew Arnstead   D. King Sturnevan

11. For whose murder are McGee and Meyer arrested in *The Long Lavender Look*?

    A. Frank Baither   C. Lew Arnstead
    B. Betsy Kapp   D. Lilo Perris

12. Who sets a trap for Travis McGee in *The Long Lavender Look*?

    A. King Sturnevan   C. Betsy Kapp
    B. Henry Perris   D. Lew Arnstead

13. Who owned Hula Marine Enterprises in *The Empty Copper Sea*?

    A. Nicky Noyes   C. John Tuckerman
    B. Hubbard Lawless   D. Van Harder

14. Who nurses McGee back to health at the end of *The Long Lavender Look*?

    A. Betsy Kapp   C. Heidi Trumbill
    B. Cathy Kerr   D. Donna Lee

15. What is the name of McGee's lawyer in *The Long Lavender Look*?

A. Heidi Trumbill   C. Isaac Longfellow
B. Leonard Sibelius   D. Smith Mercater

❖ QUIZ 8 ❖

1. Name the sheriff in *The Empty Copper Sea*.

    A. Hack Ames
    B. Nicky Noyes
    C. Colonel Boone
    D. John Tuckerman

2. What is Mia Cruikshank's occupation in *A Tan and Sandy Silence*?

    A. Airline stewardess
    B. Police officer
    C. Rancher
    D. Naval officer

3. Who kills Mary Broll in *A Tan and Sandy Silence*?

    A. Paul Dissat
    B. Travis McGee
    C. Lisa Dissat
    D. Carl Brego

4. What does the Annex refer to in *Darker Than Amber*?

   A. A bar   C. A prison
   B. A brothel   D. A church

5. How is McGee's life saved in *A Tan and Sandy Silence*?

   A. Loyal dog   C. Misfiring gun
   B. Rescued at sea   D. Emergency surgery

6. What is Arturo Taliapeloleoni's occupation in *Darker Than Amber*?

   A. Politician   C. Private investigator
   B. Bodyguard   D. Ship's steward

7. At what college did Warner Gifford work in *A Deadly Shade of Gold*?

   A. Florida A & M   C. Florida Southwestern
   B. Miami   D. Florida State

8. Who was Merrimay Lane hired to impersonate in *Darker Than Amber*?

   A. Noreen Walker   C. Jilly Blackmon
   B. Evangeline Bellemer   D. Chookie McCall

9. How was Tom Pike killed in *The Girl in the Plain Brown Wrapper*?

A. Hanged   C. Car accident
B. Shot   D. Drowned

10. Who was Nora Gardino's housemate in *A Deadly Shade of Gold*?

    A. Connie Melgar   C. Juan Drago
    B. Shaja Dobrak   D. Almah Hichin

11. Identify McGee's Cuban connection in *A Deadly Shade of Gold*.

    A. Miguel Alconedo   C. Juan Drago
    B. Connie Melgar   D. Paul Dominguez

12. Who kills Almah Hichin in *A Deadly Shade of Gold*?

    A. Travis McGee   C. Nora Gardino
    B. Paul Dominguez   D. Miguel Alconedo

13. For what is a Dormed used in *The Girl in the Plain Brown Wrapper*?

    A. Radio communica-   C. Energy
    tion   D. Sleep inducement
    B. Navigation

14. Who murders Penny Woertz in *The Girl in the Plain Brown Wrapper*?

    A. Maureen Pearson   C. Tom Pike
    B. Ben Gaffner   D. Rick Holton

15. Who tries to slip McGee a mickey in *The Girl in the Plain Brown Wrapper*?

    A. Maureen Pearson   C. Helen Bourghmer
    B. Tom Pike   D. Penny Woertz

❖ QUIZ 9 ❖

1. Who tries to ambush McGee in *The Girl in the Plain Brown Wrapper*?

   A. Rick Holton
   B. Tom Pike

   C. Dave Broon
   D. Penny Woertz

2. Near what Florida city is Ellis Esterland murdered in *Free Fall in Crimson*?

   A. Fort Lauderdale
   B. Miami

   C. Panama City
   D. Citrus City

3. What was Ellis Esterland's daughter's name in *Free Fall in Crimson*?

   A. Kathy
   B. Gail

   C. Minette
   D. Romola

4. How was Ted Lewellen killed in *The Turquoise Lament*?

    A. By drowning   C. In a motorcycle accident
    B. By shooting
                             D. In a fire

5. Who gives McGee a hallucinatory drug in *Nightmare in Pink*?

    A. Rossa Hendit   C. Robert Imber
    B. Bonita Hersch   D. Terry Drummond

6. In *Free Fall in Crimson*, who writes a letter of introduction for Travis McGee?

    A. Meyer   C. Mike Gibson
    B. Chookie McCall   D. Lysa Dean

7. Who refers McGee's client to him in *Nightmare in Pink*?

    A. Bonita Hersch   C. Howard Plummer
    B. Robert Imber   D. Mike Gibson

8. What is the name of the lawyer McGee deals with in *A Purple Place for Dying*?

    A. Michael Mazzari   C. Wally Rupert
    B. John Webb   D. Jasper Yeoman

9. What is Fred Buckleberry's occupation in *A Purple Place for Dying*?

A. Immigration officer   C. Rancher
B. Lawyer   D. County sheriff

10. To whom was Jasper Yeoman related in *A Purple Place for Dying*?

    A. Isobel Webb   C. Liz Alverson
    B. Dolores Estobar   D. Mona Yeoman

11. Identify Walter Demos from *The Dreadful Lemon Sky*.

    A. Marijuana distributor   C. Charterboat captain
    B. McGee operative   D. Police officer

12. Who kills Carrie Milligan in *The Dreadful Lemon Sky*?

    A. Fred Van Horn   C. Harry Hascomb
    B. Boo Brodey   D. Betty Joller

13. In what McGee adventure does he go to the village of Burned Wells?

    A. *Cinnamon Skin*   C. *The Turquoise Lament*
    B. *The Deep Blue Good-by* D. *A Purple Place for Dying*

14. What was Jason Breen's motive for murder in *The Dreadful Lemon Sky*?

    A. Money   C. Jealousy
    B. Love   D. Insanity

15. What is Linda Brindle's nickname in *The Turquoise Lament*?

A. Pinky

B. Sunshine

C. Heater

D. Pidge

❖ QUIZ 10 ❖

1. What was Anna Ottlo's real name in *One Fearful Yellow Eye*?

   A. Erica Stoup
   B. Heidi Browner

   C. Fredrika Gronwald
   D. Inga Steiner

2. What British incident is referred to in *Pale Gray for Guilt*?

   A. Jack the Ripper
   B. Charge of the Light Brigade

   C. Royal family spy case
   D. The Profumo sex scandal

3. In what business were Shutts, Gaylor, and Stith in *Pale Gray for Guilt*?

   A. Real estate
   B. Stock brokerage

   C. Banking
   D. Law

4. What character in *Bright Orange for the Shroud* is a fine tennis player?

   A. Boone Waxwell
   B. Wilma Ferner
   C. Debra Brown
   D. Vivian Watts

5. What is Dr. Mike Guardina's medical specialty in *Pale Gray for Guilt*?

   A. Psychiatry
   B. Cardiology
   C. Pathology
   D. Orthopedics

6. What is the name of the corporation that wanted to obtain Tush Bannon's land in *Pale Gray for Guilt*?

   A. Tech-Tex
   B. Applied Systems
   C. Southern Brokers
   D. Estates West

7. Name the lawyer who represents Janine Bannon in her attempt to recover her land in *Pale Gray for Guilt*.

   A. Rufus Wellington
   B. Andy Blackmon
   C. Chad Teasdale
   D. Skipper Goode

8. Associate Dilly Starr with a main character in *Bright Orange for the Shroud*.

   A. Boone Waxwell
   B. Travis McGee
   C. Chookie McCall
   D. Meyer

9. Who kills Wilma Ferner in *Bright Orange for the Shroud*?

   A. Boone Waxwell
   B. Debra Brown
   C. McGee
   D. Cindy Ingerfeldt

10. Identify Boone Waxwell's "nearby girl" in *Bright Orange for the Shroud*.

    A. Francine Benedict   C. Dilly Starr
    B. Cindy Ingerfeldt   D. Debra Brown

11. What character in *Bright Orange for the Shroud* is being described in the following quotation?
    "Perhaps for any man there can be something very heady about a woman totally amoral, totally without mercy, shame or softness."

    A. Debra Brown   C. Wilma Ferner
    B. Cindy Ingerfeldt   D. Francine Benedict

12. From whom does McGee get information about the whereabouts of Boone Waxwell's cash fund in *Bright Orange for the Shroud*?

    A. Cindy Ingerfeldt   C. Meyer
    B. Debra Brown   D. Boone Waxwell

13. What did McGee give Wilma Ferner and Arthur Wilkinson for a wedding gift in *Bright Orange for the Shroud*?

    A. A boat   C. Stocks
    B. Money   D. A six-pack of expensive beverages

14. What is Janice Stanyard's profession in *One Fearful Yellow Eye*?

    A. Nurse   C. Police officer
    B. Teacher   D. Accountant

15. Who is "Miss Efficiency" in *The Quick Red Fox*?

A. Dana Holtzer   C. Nancy Abbott
B. Lysa Dean   D. Kathy King

Salvage
Expert

❖ QUIZ 1 ❖

True or false?

1. "The look" as mentioned in *Dress Her in Indigo* refers to fashion modeling.

2. In *Pale Gray for Guilt*, Dusty Rose is an infamous madam.

3. The following quote from *Bright Orange for the Shroud* describes Boo Waxwell.
"That man. God, he makes my flesh crawl."

4. In *A Tan and Sandy Silence*, a Moke is a poisonous plant.

5. The Broomstick, in *The Scarlet Ruse*, is a McGeeism indicating a successful salvage.

6. In *The Scarlet Ruse*, the A-1-A refers to the combination to McGee's safe aboard his houseboat.

7. The DGI as mentioned in *The Green Ripper* refers to the Cuban secret service.

8. The dockmaster in *A Deadly Shade of Gold* is an old friend of Travis McGee.

9. As used in *The Scarlet Ruse*, B.U. refers to a person.

10. In *The Girl in the Plain Brown Wrapper*, the daily paper in Fort Courtney is called *The Gazette*.

11. "Zepp" as used in *The Scarlet Ruse* refers to a stockbroker's term.

12. Jane Lawson has two daughters in *The Scarlet Ruse*.

13. Joe True is a yacht salesman in *The Deep Blue Good-by*.

14. The character referred to as the Judge plays an *important* role in *The Dreadful Lemon Sky*.

15. Lois Atkinson's maiden name in *The Deep Blue Good-by* is Fairlea.

❖ QUIZ 2 ❖

Match the main antagonist with the Travis McGee novel in which he or she appears.

1. Anna Ottlo
2. Desmin Grizzel
3. John Tuckerman
4. Junior Allen
5. Boone Waxwell
6. Paul Dissat
7. King Sturnevan
8. Brother Persival
9. Gary Santo
10. Evan Lawrence

A. *Cinnamon Skin*
B. *One Fearful Yellow Eye*
C. *Pale Gray for Guilt*
D. *Free Fall in Crimson*
E. *The Green Ripper*
F. *The Empty Copper Sea*
G. *The Long Lavender Look*
H. *The Deep Blue Good-by*
I. *A Tan and Sandy Silence*
J. *Bright Orange for the Shroud*

❖ QUIZ 3 ❖

Match each Travis McGee title with its appropriate explanation.

 1. *Bright Orange for the Shroud*
 2. *The Green Ripper*
 3. *Nightmare in Pink*
 4. *Darker Than Amber*
 5. *The Turquoise Lament*
 6. *The Quick Red Fox*
 7. *The Empty Copper Sea*
 8. *One Fearful Yellow Eye*
 9. *A Tan and Sandy Silence*
10. *The Dreadful Lemon Sky*

A. The Grim Reaper
B. Polluted air
C. Houseboat
D. Death on the beach
E. Drug hallucination
F. Eye color
G. Look of hatred
H. The feeling of loss at
   death
 I. Sunset at sea
 J. A vixen-like woman

❖ QUIZ 4 ❖

In what book did McGee offer the following insights into his philosophy?

1. "This time they had taken one of mine. One of the displaced ones. A fellow refugee from a plastic structured culture, uninsured, unadjusted, unconvinced."

   A. *A Deadly Shade of Gold*
   B. *Bright Orange for the Shroud*
   C. *Nightmare in Pink*
   D. *Cinnamon Skin*

2. "It is difficult to put much value on something the lady has distributed all too generously."

A. *The Green Ripper*   C. *Darker Than Amber*
B. *A Purple Place for*   D. *The Empty Copper*
   Dying   *Sea*

3. "With an instant practicality, she'd changed masters."

   A. *Darker Than Amber*   C. *The Scarlet Ruse*
   B. *The Dreadful Lemon* D. *The Quick Red Fox*
      Sky

4. "I choose not to live for the insurance program, for creative selling, for suburban adjustments, for the little warm cage of kiddy-kisses..."

   A. *A Tan and Sandy Si-* C. *The Quick Red Fox*
      lence   D. *The Long Lavender*
   B. *A Deadly Shade of*   *Look*
      Gold

5. "Hesitation is a fatal disease..."

   A. *Free Fall in Crimson* C. *One Fearful Yellow*
   B. *The Green Ripper*   *Eye*
                              D. *A Tan and Sandy Si-*
                                 lence

❖ QUIZ 5 ❖

1. Identify the term COBÁ as referred to in *Cinnamon Skin*.

   A. Mayan Ruins
   B. South American
   dance

   C. Mexican herb
   D. Inca dialect

2. In what book other than *The Quick Red Fox* does Gabe Marchman appear?

   A. *The Turquoise Lament*
   B. *Pale Gray for Guilt*

   C. *Cinnamon Skin*
   D. *One Fearful Yellow Eye*

3. In the *The Scarlet Ruse*, what is a thin?

   A. A European cigarette
   B. A flawed stamp

   C. A military strategy
   D. A government policy

4. In *The Deep Blue Good-by*, what is Junior Allen's first name?

    A. Chutney   C. Ambrose
    B. Dirk   D. Lewis

5. In what fictional Florida county does *The Long Lavender Look* take place?

    A. Cypress   C. Miami
    B. Orlando   D. Everglades

6. What economic prediction does Meyer make in *The Green Ripper*?

    A. Anarchy   C. Stagnation
    B. Boom times   D. Collapse

7. What poet is quoted in *The Empty Copper Sea*?

    A. Longfellow   C. Shelley
    B. Keats   D. Thoreau

8. In *Darker Than Amber*, what did "a very talented oldtime con man" teach McGee?

    A. Car theft   C. Picking pockets
    B. Acting drunk   D. Impersonations

9. To whom does McGee attribute the following quotation in *A Deadly Shade of Gold*?
"The expense is damnable, the position ridiculous, the pleasure fleeting."

A. Winston Churchill   C. Buckminster Fuller
B. Bertrand Russell   D. Samuel Johnson

10. What is being referred to in question 9?

    A. Politics   C. Money
    B. Sex   D. Warfare

11. Name the state attorney in *The Girl in the Plain Brown Wrapper*.

    A. Dave Broon   C. Tom Pike
    B. Ben Gaffner   D. Rick Holton

12. Name the director of the two films mentioned in *Free Fall in Crimson*.

    A. Peter Kesner   C. Lysa Dean
    B. Desmin Grizzel   D. Sarah Isson

13. In *The Turquoise Lament*, to what does the term New People refer?

    A. Bureaucrats   C. Persons who are
    B. Illegal aliens   incapable of being
                            alone
                         D. Immigrants

14. In *Nightmare in Pink*, to what type of dog is McGee referring in this quotation?
    "This is the most desperate breed..."

    A. Doberman   C. Poodle
    B. German shepherd   D. Collie

15. What is Madeline Houser's occupation in *A Purple Place for Dying*?

A. College professor   C. Airline stewardess
B. Geologist   D. Forest ranger

❖ QUIZ 6 ❖

1. Who was killed aboard McGee's houseboat in *The Dreadful Lemon Sky*?

    A. Carrie Milligan
    B. Cindy Birdsong
    C. Susan Dobrovsky
    D. Joanna Freeler

2. According to Meyer in *One Fearful Yellow Eye*, who was the one who got away?

    A. Susan Kemmer
    B. Heidi Trumbill
    C. Mildred Shottle-hauster
    D. Janice Stanyard

3. What unusual hobby does Brandy Davis have in *Cinnamon Sky*?

    A. Autographs
    B. Bottle caps
    C. Travel posters
    D. Collects unusual boat names

4. Who are Warner Housell and Rowland Service in *Cinnamon Skin*?

   A. Government agents   C. Private detectives
   B. Mobsters   D. Naval officers

5. What was Evan Lawrence's stepmother's name in *Cinnamon Skin*?

   A. Coralita   C. Lisa
   B. Jenny   D. Kathy

6. In *Cinnamon Skin*, which of the following characters is associated with Annie Renzetti?

   A. Evan Lawrence   C. Howard Pine
   B. Norma Evans   D. Brandy Davis

7. Name Lysa Dean's boyfriend in *The Quick Red Fox*.

   A. Sam Edgewood   C. Paul Mantee
   B. Ben Godwin   D. Carl Abelle

8. What city is being described by the following quote from *The Quick Red Fox*?
   "A bored kid built a shiny little model city with his new kit and when it was finished he gave it one hell of a kick and spewed big hunks of it..."

   A. Phoenix   C. Las Vegas
   B. New York   D. Los Angeles

9. What was Nancy Abbott's medical problem in *The Quick Red Fox*?

   A. Diabetes   C. Ulcer
   B. Drug addiction   D. Alcoholism

10. Where did Sonny Catton die in *The Quick Red Fox*?

    A. California   C. Georgia
    B. Texas   D. Mexico

11. What were both Bogen and Ives in *The Quick Red Fox*?

    A. Blackmailers   C. McGee's friends
    B. Undercover agents   D. Murder victims

12. Of the following characters from *The Quick Red Fox*, which one was not a participant in a blackmail scheme?

    A. Carl Abelle   C. Bobby Blessing
    B. Sonny Catton   D. Nancy Abbott

13. Cathy Kerr appears in *The Scarlet Ruse*. In what other McGee adventure does she appear?

    A. *Dress Her in Indigo*   C. *The Deep Blue Good-*
    B. *The Dreadful Lemon*   *by*
        Sky   D. *Pale Gray for Guilt*

14. What character in *The Scarlet Ruse* spent time in a reformatory?

    A. Jane Lawson   C. Mary McDermit
    B. Frank Sprenger   D. Cathy Kerr

15. To what do the terms "pulled perf" and "gum disturbance" refer in *The Scarlet Ruse*?

    A. Valuable paintings   C. Geological strata
    B. Precious stones   D. Stamps

❖ QUIZ 7 ❖

1. In what business is William Callowell in *The Deep Blue Good-by*?

   A. Banking
   B. Import-export

   C. Aerospace
   D. Construction

2. Whom does McGee intimidate into disclosing important information in *The Deep Blue Good-by*?

   A. Junior Allen
   B. Lois Atkinson

   C. George Brell
   D. David Berry

3. Identify Buttercup from *The Long Lavender Look*.

   A. A horse
   B. A dog

   C. A boat
   D. A girlfriend of McGee's

4. What is the name of the religious fringe group that McGee encounters in *The Green Ripper*?

   A. Disciples of Faith
   B. The Cross Bearers
   C. Church of the Apocrypha
   D. Church of the Chosen

5. Who is being described by the following quote from *The Deep Blue Good-by*?
   "He was a skull-cracker, two steps away from the cave."

   A. Shane Frawley
   B. Hugo Essen
   C. Junior Allen
   D. George Brell

6. What are Geraldine Kimmey, Linda Featherman, and Donna Lee in *The Long Lavender Look*?

   A. Call girls
   B. Murder victims
   C. Girlfriends of McGee
   D. Undercover police officers

7. All of the following characters appear in *The Green Ripper* except one. Name this character.

   A. Vance M'Gruder
   B. Billy Maxwell
   C. Brother Titus
   D. Robert E. Kline

8. What does 68-17-6 represent in *The Long Lavender Look*?

   A. Safe combination
   B. Computer access code
   C. Map coordinates
   D. Boxer's fight record

9. Name the editor of the Cypress County newspaper in *The Long Lavender Look*.

   A. Foster Goss
   B. Gena Waterman
   C. Chad Jones
   D. Sam Essex

10. What is a *morgen* as used in *The Green Ripper*?

   A. Currency
   B. A land measurement
   C. A parliamentary body
   D. An antique car

11. From whom did Meyer acquire letters of financial reference in *The Empty Copper Sea*?

   A. Devlin Boggs
   B. Emmett Albritton
   C. John Tuckerman
   D. Hubbard Lawless

12. Who was Georgi Markov as mentioned in *The Green Ripper*?

   A. A McGee alias
   B. A KGB agent
   C. A Bulgarian defector
   D. A Russian diplomat

13. Identify Tide Watch from *The Empty Copper Sea*.

   A. A luxury yacht
   B. A painting
   C. A condominium
   D. A naval radar

14. Who had McGee been crewing for as *The Empty Copper Sea* opens?

   A. Duke Davis
   B. Meyer
   C. Chookie McCall
   D. Van Harder

15. Where do McGee and Meyer stay during their investigation in *The Empty Copper Sea*?

A. Aboard McGee's   C. Hotel
   houseboat   D. Private home
B. Yacht club

❖ QUIZ 8 ❖

1. What was Ralph Stennenmacher's occupation in *The Empty Copper Sea*?

   A. Insurance agent
   B. Police officer

   C. Tugboat captain
   D. Politician

2. He's a Canadian financier in *A Tan and Sandy Silence*. Who is he?

   A. Harry Broll
   B. Paul Dissat

   C. McDill Lee
   D. Dennis Waterbury

3. In *Darker Than Amber*, what is a "fishbowl"?

   A. A commercial aquarium
   B. A slang term for drugs

   C. A nude dancing effect
   D. Police surveillance

4. How much money did McGee receive for the Menterez collection in *A Deadly Shade of Gold*?

   A. $55,000   C. $162,500
   B. $105,000   D. $1 million

5. What is the name of Tom Pike's investment company in *The Girl in the Plain Brown Wrapper*?

   A. LandScapes   C. United Estates
   B. Acre's Unlimited D. Development Unlimited

6. Who is being described in the following quotation from *Darker Than Amber*?
   "Her twelve years on the track had coarsened her beyond any hope of salvage."

   A. Evangeline Bellemer   C. Merrimay Lane
   B. Jane Stussland   D. Adele Whitney

7. Who was the leader of the American Crusade in *A Deadly Shade of Gold*?

   A. Girdon Face   C. Carlos Menterez
   B. Cal Tomberlin   D. Arista

8. In what profession are Folmer, Hardahee, and Kranz in *The Girl in the Plain Brown Wrapper*?

   A. Accounting   C. The military
   B. Law   D. Medicine

9. From what source did McGee obtain information concerning Tami Western in *Darker Than Amber*?

   A. Noreen Walker   C. Police files
   B. Meyer   D. Sam Dickey

10. What poet is quoted in *Darker Than Amber*?

    A. Byron   C. Shakespeare
    B. Auden   D. Milton

11. From what university did Paul Dissat graduate in *A Tan and Sandy Silence*?

    A. M.I.T.   C. The Sorbonne
    B. Florida State   D. McGill

12. Who is being described in the following quote from *A Deadly Shade of Gold*?
    "... was a random guy, a big, restless, reckless, lantern-jawed ex-marine, a brawler, a wencher, a two-fisted drinker."

    A. Travis McGee   C. Meyer
    B. Sam Taggart   D. Clint Lewis

13. Who recommended Travis McGee to Ron Esterland in *Free Fall in Crimson*?

    A. Meyer   C. Aggie Sloane
    B. The Alabama Tiger   D. Sarah Issom

14. Whom did McGee intimidate into giving valuable information concerning Carlos Menterez in *A Deadly Shade of Gold*?

    A. Sam Taggart   C. Miguel Alconedo
    B. Gabe Day   D. Almah Hichin

❖ QUIZ 9 ❖

1. What are Gavin and Donnie in *Free Fall In Crimson*?

   A. Lawyers
   B. Doctors
   C. Bodyguards
   D. Stuntmen

2. Who killed Jean Norman and Joya Murphy-Wheeler in *Free Fall in Crimson*?

   A. Ted Blaylock
   B. Peter Kesner
   C. McGee
   D. Desmin Grizzel

3. What is unusual about Coop's airplane in *The Turquoise Lament*?

   A. Old WWII bomber
   B. Russian built
   C. Hijacked to Cuba
   D. Built from a kit

4. Name Meyer's private nurse in *The Turquoise Lament*.

    A. Ella Morse   C. Chookie McCall
    B. Alice Alasega   D. Linda Brindle

5. What institution of higher learning is mentioned in *Nightmare in Pink*?

    A. Pratt Institute   C. U.C.L.A.
    B. Harvard   D. University of Maryland

6. Identify Nina Gibson's financé in *Nightmare in Pink*.

    A. Travis McGee   C. Charles Armister
    B. Robert Imber   D. Howard Plummer

7. From what language is the following proverb taken in *The Turquoise Lament*?
"A bore is a person who deprives you of solitude without providing you with company."

    A. German   C. English
    B. French   D. Spanish

8. Name Charles Armister's personal secretary in *Nightmare in Pink*.

    A. Bonita Hersch   C. Constance Thatcher
    B. Nina Gibson   D. Terry Drummond

9. What is Beatrice Bowie's nickname in *Dress Her in Indigo*?

    A. Bix   C. Runner
    B. Sunshine   D. BB

10. What do George Raub, John Benjamin, and Doris Wright-son have in common in *Nightmare in Pink*?

    A. Murder victims
    B. Witnessess on grand jury
    C. McGee's friends
    D. Hospital inmates

11. What is the term Currency Curtain associated with in *Nightmare in Pink*?

    A. International drug trade
    B. Devaluation
    C. Counterfeit money
    D. Security by wealth

12. Who is being described by the following quote from *Nightmare in Pink*?
    "Her heart was cold as a stone at the bottom of a mountain lake."

    A. Rousa Hendit
    B. Terry Drummond
    C. Nina Gibson
    D. Bonita Hersch

13. What are the three unholy McGees as referred to in *Nightmare in Pink*?

    A. Three ex-friends
    B. A philosophy
    C. An economic condition
    D. A political statement

14. Identify the speaker from this quote from *Nightmare in Pink*.
    "I've spent my life in the major leagues."

    A. Terry Drummond
    B. Travis McGee
    C. Meyer
    D. Bonita Hersch

15. To what does Desert Gate refer in *The Quick Red Fox*?

    A. A cemetery   C. A marina
    B. A hotel   D. A trailer park

❖ QUIZ 10 ❖

1. What character in *Dress Her in Indigo* is a graduate of the Stanford University Business School?

    A. Meyer
    B. Beatrice Bowie
    C. Rebecca Harrison
    D. Enelio Fuentes

2. What is a "cronkie" as referred to in *A Purple Place for Dying*?

    A. Police slang
    B. Illegal immigrant
    C. A small power boat
    D. An amateur water skier

3. What is Bruce Bundy's profession in *Dress Her in Indigo*?

    A. Interior decorator
    B. Set designer
    C. Mercenary
    D. College professor

4. Who attempted to get McGee to participate in the marijuana smuggling business in *The Dreadful Lemon Sky*?

    A. Harry Hascomb   C. Walter Demos
    B. Carrie Milligan   D. Boo Brodey

5. Who is illegimate in *A Purple Place for Dying*?

    A. Jasper Yeoman   C. Fran Weaver
    B. Isobel Webb   D. Dolores Estobar

6. At what marina does McGee dock his houseboat in *The Dreadful Lemon Sky*?

    A. SeaView   C. Westway Harbor
    B. Master-Dock   D. AnchorAway

7. Identify the character from the description in *Dress Her in Indigo*.
"... archeology major from the University of New Mexico."

    A. Burt Koontz   C. Wally McLeen
    B. Beatrice Bowie   D. Elena Amparo

8. Who is being described in the following quote from *A Purple Place for Dying*?
"He's sixty now. You talk about feudal. . . . He don't have five friends in the world..."

    A. McGee's father   C. John Webb
    B. Jasper Yeoman   D. Wally Rupert

9. How much money did Carrie Milligan leave with McGee for safekeeping in *The Dreadful Lemon Sky*?

    A. $54,000   C. $104,000
    B. $94,200   D. $250,000

10. To what does GLC 085-14-0277 refer in *One Fearful Yellow Eye*?

    A. A safe combination   C. An annuity policy
    B. A passport number   D. A serial number on a
                                             stock certificate

11. What is Tush Bannon's real first name in *Pale Gray for Guilt*?

    A. Grammacy   C. Chucker
    B. Zebulon   D. Brantley

12. Who is president of the Shawana National Bank in *Pale Gray for Guilt*?

    A. Whitt Sanders   C. D. J. Carbee
    B. Bunny Burgoon   D. Freddy Hazzard

13. Who was Frank Durkin's girlfriend in *Bright Orange for the Shroud*?

    A. Chookie McCall   C. Francine Benedict
    B. Vivian Watts   D. Debra Brown

14. What is the name of the company stock that McGee cons Gary Santo into buying in, in *Pale Gray for Guilt*?

A. Southern Textiles   C. AgraTech

B. Longhaul, Inc.   D. Fletcher Industries

15. Who or what is being described in *Pale Gray for Guilt* as "Big Voice of the Big Bay"?

A. A coast guard rescue team   C. Illegal drug traffickers

B. A disc jockey   D. A local sports announcer

Answers

Apprentice Detective

QUIZ 1

1. C	6. C
2. C	7. D
3. A	8. C
4. A	9. D
5. C	10. D

QUIZ 2

1. A	6. A
2. D	7. C
3. C	8. B
4. B	9. A
5. D	10. A

QUIZ 3

1. False	9. True
2. True	10. False
3. False	11. False
4. True	12. False
5. False	13. True
6. False	14. False
7. False	15. False
8. True	

QUIZ 4

1. *Cinnamon Skin*
2. *The Green Ripper*
3. *The Dreadful Lemon Sky*
4. *The Scarlet Ruse*
5. *The Long Lavender Look*
6. *The Girl In The Plain*
   Brown Wrapper
7. *One Fearful Yellow Eye*
8. *Bright Orange For The*
   Shroud
9. *The Quick Red Fox*
10. *Nightmare In Pink*

QUIZ 5

1. D	9. D
2. C	10. C
3. C	11. C
4. D	12. A
5. D	13. A
6. D	14. C
7. D	15. A
8. A	

QUIZ 6

1. B	9. A
2. A	10. C
3. D	11. D
4. B	12. D
5. B	13. A
6. B	14. B
7. B	15. A
8. C	

QUIZ 7

1. A	9. A
2. D	10. C
3. A	11. A
4. A	12. C
5. C	13. D
6. A	14. B
7. D	15. C
8. D	

QUIZ 8

1. C	9. C
2. C	10. D
3. B	11. A
4. A	12. D
5. D	13. B
6. A	14. D
7. B	15. C
8. A	

QUIZ 9

1. B	9. D
2. B	10. C
3. D	11. C
4. D	12. B
5. A	13. D
6. A	14. B
7. D	15. D
8. C	

QUIZ 10

1. A	9. C
2. D	10. B
3. C	11. B
4. C	12. D
5. B	13. C
6. A	14. A
7. C	15. A & D
8. C	

Super Sleuth

QUIZ 1

1. False	9. False
2. False	10. False
3. False	11. False
4. False	12. False
5. True	13. False
6. True	14. True
7. False	15. False
8. False	

QUIZ 2

1. A	6. I
2. G	7. D
3. C	8. J
4. H	9. E
5. B	10. F

QUIZ 3

1. A & H	6. I
2. J	7. G
3. D	8. E
4. F	9. C
5. H	10. A

QUIZ 4

1. B	6. I
2. D	7. G
3. F	8. E
4. H	9. C
5. J	10. A

QUIZ 5

1. A	9. D
2. B	10. D
3. D	11. A
4. D	12. D
5. B	13. D
6. D	14. B
7. B	15. A
8. A	

QUIZ 6

1. A	9. C
2. C	10. A
3. A	11. C
4. C	12. B
5. C	13. B
6. B	14. C
7. C	15. C
8. A	

QUIZ 7

1. B
2. A & B
3. C
4. D
5. B
6. A
7. A
8. A
9. B
10. D
11. A
12. B
13. B
14. C
15. B

QUIZ 8

1. A
2. A
3. A
4. A
5. B
6. D
7. C
8. B
9. A
10. B
11. D
12. D
13. D
14. C
15. D

QUIZ 9

1. A
2. D
3. D
4. C
5. A
6. D
7. D
8. A
9. D
10. B
11. A
12. C
13. D
14. C
15. D

QUIZ 10

1. C	9. A
2. D	10. B
3. B	11. A
4. D	12. A
5. C	13. D
6. A	14. A
7. A	15. A
8. A	

Salvage Expert

QUIZ 1

1. False
2. False
3. True
4. False
5. False
6. False
7. True
8. False
9. False
10. False
11. False
12. True
13. True
14. False
15. True

QUIZ 2

1. B
2. D
3. F
4. H.
5. J
6. I
7. G
8. E
9. C
10. A

QUIZ 3

1. C	6. J
2. A	7. I
3. E	8. G
4. F	9. D
5. H	10. B

QUIZ 4

1. A	4. B
2. C	5. D
3. A	

QUIZ 5

1. A	9. D
2. A	10. B
3. B	11. B
4. C	12. A
5. A	13. C
6. D	14. C
7. D	15. C
8. B	

QUIZ 6

1. D	9. D
2. B	10. C
3. D	11. A
4. A	12. C
5. A	13. C
6. C	14. C
7. D	15. D
8. C	

QUIZ 7

1. D	9. A
2. C	10. B
3. B	11. B
4. C	12. C
5. C	13. B
6. A	14. A
7. A	15. C
8. D	

QUIZ 8

1. A	8. B
2. D	9. A
3. C	10. B
4. C	11. D
5. D	12. B
6. A	13. D
7. A	14. D

QUIZ 9

1. C	9. A
2. D	10. D
3. D	11. D
4. A	12. D
5. A	13. B
6. D	14. A
7. D	15. D
8. A	

QUIZ 10

1. D	9. B
2. A	10. C
3. B	11. D
4. D	12. A
5. D	13. A
6. C	14. D
7. A	15. B
8. D	

21
Adventures

John D. MacDonald's
TRAVIS McGEE SERIES

Travis McGee—star of twenty-one novels, every one
as good as the last—part rebel, part philosopher,
and every inch his own man. He is a rugged,
Florida beach bum with a special knack
for helping friends in trouble—or
avenging their deaths.

"McGee has become part of our national
fabric." *Seattle Post Intellegencer*